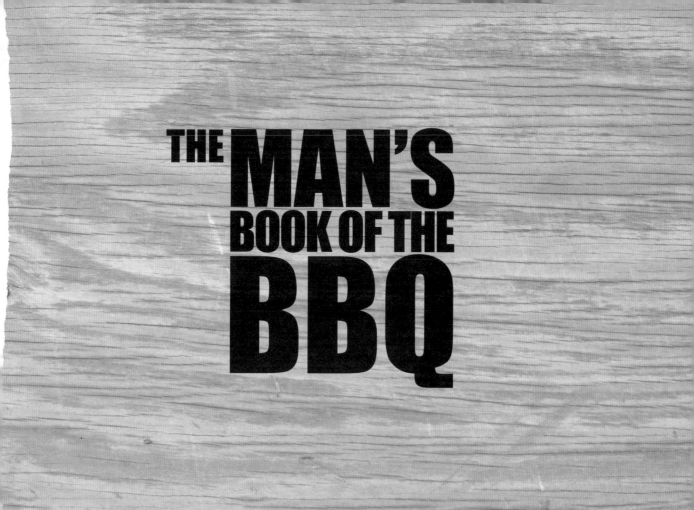

THE MAN'S
BOOK OF THE
BBQ

THE MAN'S
BOOK OF THE
BBQ

A CELEBRATION OF FULL-ON, FLAME-ON, MACHO COOKING!

Brendan McGinley

spruce

An Hachette UK Company
www.hachette.co.uk

First published in Great Britain in 2011 by Spruce,
a division of Octopus Publishing Group Ltd
Endeavour House, 189 Shaftesbury Avenue, London
WC2H 8JY. www.octopusbooks.usa.com

Copyright © Octopus Publishing Group Ltd 2011

Distributed in the U.S. and Canada by Octopus Books USA:
c/o Hachette Book Group, 237 Park Avenue, New York, NY 10017

Brendan McGinley asserts the moral right to be identified as
the author of this work.

ISBN 978-1-846-01391-1

A CIP catalogue record for this book is available from the
British Library

Printed and bound in China

10 9 8 7 6 5 4 3 2 1

This book is a work of satire and as such nothing it contains in any way
purports to be factual, therefore the publisher, packager, and author cannot
accept liability for any resulting injury or damage to either property or person,
whether direct or consequential and howsoever arising, incurred as a result of
using information featured in this book. The characters mentioned in the book
are entirely fictitious, and bear no relation whatsoever to people, objects or
places depicted in images accompanying the text; any resemblance to any
person living or dead within the text is entirely coincidental. All cooking times
are approximate as cooking times may be affected by such factors as altitude,
wind, outside temperature, and desired doneness.

CONTENTS

AN INTRODUCTION FROM THE AUTHOR, WHO HAS NEVER LEARNED TO KNOW BETTER

Within these pages, you will find a guide to basic barbecuing techniques, why donning a fancy apron makes a real man, and how to kill your enemies using only brown sugar. One of those is a lie, which I've replaced with pictures of gimmicky grills and exemplary backyard chefs. You will also encounter some of my favourite recipes, made fancier by my own personal touches—mango here, curry there, and dolphin everywhere, if you can get it freshly grated.

My advice to you is demand much of your faculties while you have them. You're going to end up weak and indolent no matter what you do. In fact, you could use some good, rich beef to

Grilling in the rain is a great way to ensure moist barbecue... maybe too moist. Admirable dedication, though!

Sneaking a meal off your neighbor's grill is an excellent way to save money and cleanup.

build muscle for the declining years. Do you think if you only eat celery, you won't grow old? Wrong, because celery is very low in calories, but extremely high in regret, which ages a man even faster than having children (one of nature's richest sources of gray hair).

If you're going to die after an extended period of decay, you might as well have some fun along the way. And by "fun" I mean "hedonism."

For me, this is erotica.

01 THE BBQ—FROM CAVEMAN TO METROMAN

The oldest cave drawings are ochre, clay, and ash—meaning at least half of human art and writing can be credited to barbecue and its longtime partner, fire. If the clay was from some type of primitive pig roast, you're talking the full span of human progress hiding in juicy baby-back ribs.

That's why we men cling so closely to our raw caveman instincts. We're not against progress, we're just preserving the original traditions that eventually launched the naked ape to the moon. It's imperative in all human discovery and adventure to find new and interesting things, and spit-roast them.

stop ogling her;
she's everyone's
great-grandmother.

ESSENCE HARNESSING THE POWER OF BARBECUE FOR CHANGES IN YOUR LIFE TODAY!

The term barbecue comes from the Arawak word *barbacoa*, which means "barbecue." Obviously the Arawak Indians weren't the first people to invent it, else they would have conquered the world or perhaps died of heart disease before they could pass the term on.

Barbecue is a powerful force in the universe, and must be wielded responsibly. Too many societies have collapsed because their only repast was beef, butter, and beer, which sounds like a great Friday night, but do it every day and it loses its worth.

BARBECUERS ANONYMOUS

Barbecue teaches us to enjoy life not only in self-indulgence, but in self-denial. Once you see the interstitial periods between barbecue as necessary and equally savory, you will gain full mastery over mouth-watering. Or you will be found wanting, and it will kill you. Either way: we're all better off.

God's own barbecue

There's an old truism: hunger is the best sauce. This is true, but should be qualified: in conjunction with barbecue.

If a culture develops barbecue too early, lesser inventions like writing and the wheel go ignored.

CREATION LET THERE BE LIGHT—APPLIED JUDICIOUSLY AND EVENLY

The first barbecue is difficult to place. Some describe how the meal sprang fully formed from Zeus's stomach. Others say Zeus took the shape of a cow to seduce a woman, but was slaughtered by her hungry husband. In any case, they're both a revision of *The Epic of Gilgamesh*, in which the eponymous Epic and his sidekick Enkidu butcher the Bull of Heaven.

That's right. The world's oldest story is about drinking, scoring high-quality tail, and getting into trouble with your buddy. It also illustrates the necessity of growing up, facing mortality, and finding your place in the community.

THE TRUE MAN'S RELIGION

Barbecue, therefore, is at the core of modern civilization. It tames wild men and completes the hearts of heroes. It's not just a way to kill a Sunday afternoon; it's the heart of the world's oldest religion, which will guide you to a balanced life. Historically speaking, most gods demand a sacrifice of "burnt offerings" (read: "barbecue"), which—in a surprise to

These deities also frequently require olive oil and wine. It turns out people will bring you everything good in life if you tell them it's for God. Many religions demand celibacy from their priests, meaning at some point, to prevent suspicion, they denied themselves one of life's pleasures, and sex lost to barbecue.

Once you've reached khef-a-tet, the 19th level of barbecuing, a white lotus will unfold in your mind, and you will be able to resist the allure of smoked meats until you reach a transcendental state of hunger.

using every part of the animal is easy when i tastes like barbecue sau

Holy mackerel! Look at the size of those, well... holey mackerel.

Interestingly, barbecue heaven saves costs by doubling as cow hell.

GRILLIOLITHIC
THE AGE OF BARBECUE

You have to figure at least one Tyrannosaurus Rex was struck by lightning. Can you imagine how delicious that must have been? And no people around to eat it. Since the dawn of archeology, man has dreamed of eating T-Rex. Fred Flintstone so craved Rex ribs, he upset his granite pedi-push car to obtain them.

Recent evidence suggests the lizard king was a scavenger rather than a hunter, which offends most people because then it would taste gamey. Ideally, you want to eat vegetarians, not carnivores, and definitely not hyenas, trust me. I tried hyena once on expedition in whatever country hyenas live in (let's say it was Prussia). It tasted like an old woman had eaten an all-newspaper diet and then died of a broken heart. That's also why I don't make steak out of spinsters anymore. Besides, the marbling on middle-aged playboys is so much richer.

GRILLING DARWIN

All nature comes down to "eat or be eaten." Some creatures, like plants or mantises looking to get laid, encourage their own consumption.

You'd set your own mother as bait for a chance to eat that.

The pig, for example, has flourished on six continents with its evolutionary advantage of tasting delicious. Sure, it might be smart enough to forage for itself, and even score the good truffles, but what behooves the

In addition to selling his soul to Satan, Faust was the proprietor of a successful chain of barbecue restaurants.

individual doesn't necessarily promulgate the species in the same numbers. Everything dies. But if we can respect that death by making it as meaningful (read: tasty) as possible, then, like Faust, we can scream to a silent night sky, "I have defied you, random existence! Look what I have made! I, who, while living, have guided this creature from the world with dignity and delicious saffron seasoning! I have conquered death and made it beautiful and noble!"

SPIT-ROASTING THE UNIVERSE

The first barbecue was meat held over the flame in bare hands, but that turned out even uglier than a drink with frat boys. Undaunted, people put meat on sticks and turned them until they were scorched all over and raw inside; humanity's first cooked meal was rotisserie. In fact, the last meal will be rotisserie. If you look at it astronomically, *all* meals are rotisserie.

One day the cosmic dance will end when hungry black holes decide our planet is ready to be eaten. At the end of everything, the universe will stop turning, shove all that ever was into its hungry maw, and turn itself inside out for the rotation to begin again. It's…it's rather beautiful, all told.

Bacon, bakin'.

WHOOPS! GOODBYE APPENDIX

The discovery of fire brought an end to the Golden Age of Diseases, and the noble career of the appendix. If you people had the decency to feed your children raw meat, they'd develop throbbing, strong appendices that would make them immune to toxins like botulism and reality TV, hungry for hard work, and incapable of graffiti.

Early man wandered the landscape, bumping into things, stabbing them, and eating them if they weren't rocks, although he'd break that rule for halite (aka salt). It only took three generations to learn you can't get blood from a stone, but you can get salt—the world's first rub.

USE YOUR BRAIN

Barbecue evolved much like—and indeed, is responsible for—the cortices of the human brain. Just as your lizard parts lurk below conscious thought, so too do indirect heat and smoking form the base upon which the more subtle methods of rubbing and basting grew.

By the way, the brain needs no marinating, but you have to cook it just right or it gets very rubbery. Nor should you undercook, lest you ingest the creature's thoughts and inherit stupefying memories, such as grazing and being eaten by yourself. It's all very solipsistic, which I don't recommend unless you're making southern French cuisine.

Barbecue remained unrefined until the rise of agrarian culture 6,000 or 40,000 years ago, when beef was finally plentiful and someone was home all day to put all the work into it.

There was a time in human history when this was literally the fiscal equivalent of a mountain range made of gold.

Smart drinks are increasingly popular.

THE FUTURE OUR DESTINY ON THE RACK

The future of barbecue is appropriately smoky, but one day the sauce of knowledge will slather our tender culinary repertoire. Barbecue brings people together, even vegetarians, who like to glaze soy and pretend it's food. Barbecue has gone global, and one day all humanity will be united under its grease-stained banner.

That's when the aliens will get us. You thought crop circles and blood-drained cattle were the work of two drunks and a shadowy government agency? Don't be silly. The more obvious answer is extraterrestrial intelligences have acquired barbecue and are setting the table. I don't know about you, but I can think of no end more noble than slowly marinating under barbecue technology that's light-years ahead of ours. Perhaps a laser will instantaneously peel the steaming meat from our bones. What an honor that would be!

DRIPPING FAT

Or perhaps we'll simply destroy ourselves with some sort of barbecue-based campaign—I'm thinking obesity, deforestation, and depletion of natural resources like coal and propane. Millions of years from now, magpie archeologists will unearth our scant remaining bones, and say, "Can you imagine how delicious that must have been? And we weren't around to eat it."

And so, life goes on.

How disappointing to finally decipher the crop circle's cryptic message: "Mastercard accepted here."

02 BARBECUE BONANZA!

There are lots of grills out there, some with even wackier methods than the various fuels and fires we describe elsewhere in this book. But none is truly better than the other, unless you have a pit spread with banana leaves and 16 hours for some casual smoking. You can't beat that no matter how hard you try. And certainly, the rust-bombs and toppling semi-pits halfway through this chapter are inferior to every method except a lighter with a fervent prayer.

You know what? I take it back. You can rate a grill, and this chapter looks at a whole spectrum of them. Learn to appreciate their nuances so you can select the right one for your lifestyle. In my case, I like a light, portable aluminum number to suit my life of crime.

Grills in the wild live in matriarchal clans of up to 30. Scientists are debating whether to refer to them as flocks, prides, or just a really good time.

BUILT LIKE A BRICK SMOKEHOUSE
WHAT HAPPENED TO THE CHIMNEY, DADDY?

A brick barbecue is a great way to prepare your food. The natural brickiness of these formations traps the elemental form of heat known as *phlogiston*, imparting the meal with the finest aromas of 17th century pseudoscience. Another benefit: the lack of chimney guarantees you won't encounter Dick van Dyke overwringing a Cockney accent.

Such grills are also an excellent way to educate your children. Observe the baby being permitted to touch the hot stove. What ho! He won't soon try that again! That'll teach him to trust his betters as he learns about his world. And say, is his mother the loveliest thing on two legs, or what? Whuh-oh! Dad's in his undershirt! That means a fight, and that, in turn, means it's time to skedaddle. You can't enjoy barbecue with a fist in your stomach. Unless, obviously, you barbecued and ate a fist, but I don't recommend that. The scant portion of meat isn't enough pay-off for the cooking time involved in softening the tendons.

Meanwhile, check out that other family in glorious technicolor. I think they may be homeless. Laugh at them with me, won't you, dear reader? Well, not at them, that would be cruel, but at their circumstances. Thank God we're better off than they! Whew!

Anyway: brick. It's sturdy, reassuring, and it's my preferred grill. I like a nice clay-shale hardburn composite brick, but you're free to use anything up to and including a 20 per cent pure silicate component. Let your freak flag fly, man! Barbecue doesn't judge.

If a child cannot build his own fire by schooling age, he will be cast out of the clan.

This ambiguous gathering is a Hopper painting come to life.

PECULIARITY HIGH, HATTED, AND TEMPTING FATE

Idiosyncrasy is an important factor in any barbecue rig, and you should certainly choose one that reflects your personality as a grillmeister. Even though I live in a humble yurt with what few possessions I can craft from the remains of my kills, my grilling persona is G.J. Snazzy Bling-Blang. The G.J. stands for "Grill Jockey," which in turn stands for "Super-Cool Dude!!!!" (the number of exclamation marks is important.) Snazzy, because I have no idea what that means, much like I usually have no idea what I'm cooking, and Bling, because my grill is made of solid gold, a soft metal which cannot support much weight under heat. The Blang is silent. All of which lets people know that when they come over to my house for a barbecue, they'll be laughing either with me or at me, but the food will be delicious.

A TILE TOO FAR

Nevertheless, it is possible to take such personalization too far, to the point where it interferes with your functionality, such as these enterprising youths have done. Not only is their grill at an inappropriate angle for cooking, but

their tinder is too green, and stored in a place where it could ignite. Also, they seem to have put a roof on their car. I don't know if you noticed that giant roof. Felted and all. No wonder they laughed at the suggestion of accelerants.

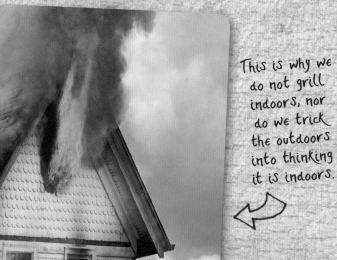

This is why we do not grill indoors, nor do we trick the outdoors into thinking it is indoors.

It all amounts to a car you don't want to drive, a grill you don't want to use, kindling you won't have, a fire you can't put out, and burgers that—hold on. Mmmmm! say, you guys, these are really good—what's your secret?

Really? The slate roof?

wow.

TINKERS, TRAVELERS, AND TRAILER TRASH

Don't let your kids near this moldy pile of cinderblock. I'd rather do my cooking on a half-completed Jenga puzzle. But hey, at least the inefficiently escaping heat will blister your shins as you tend the grill! Even if you have a frontispiece for that contraption, the heat source is too low, and you're picking pine needles out of the food. Shenanigans!

Just look at that barrel! "I eat your food!" he chomps in a cartoony voice. "More food in my mouth, pleeze!" I'd give my burger a tetanus shot before sending it off to die in his tummy.

Here's one suited to an evening on the wild frontiers of a wood near you. Food cooks itself while you tend to other camp duties, like attracting bears, fleeing bears, or being killed by bears. How do people in temperate climes venture unprepared towards death without bears? (Or as we call 'em in the states, land-sharks.)

A venerable old-timer who has survived endless summers and typhoons. Imagine the armies of shrimp who have asked me to refer to them as prawns before they are steamed to death in those baskets. When you're done, you can flip one over for use as a steel drum. Brother, you've got yourself a summer feast.

A LITTLE TOO PERFECT
(APART FROM THE POISONED DOG)

Remember that scene in the epic *A Wrinkle in Time*, where the Overmind regulated and synchronized everything? No? Good, because I never finished that book either. But I hear tell the children in that world pat the dog in even, regular strokes, every man has his haircut trimmed that morning, the propane (of course) grill is always set to 375°, and mosquitoes wouldn't dream of interrupting the perfectly lovely day.

But what. Is. Wrong with. THAT. WATERMELON? Who chopped that lovely fruit into uneven portions? There are protocols that must be obeyed here! We're in propane land! No, it's all gone wrong—destroy it all! Wipe it out! Start over again! These imperfections must be culled, and they have infected all the other elements with their sloppiness.

SAY, WAIT A MINUTE...

Here's an idea—maybe next time you could take the minor annoyances along with the grand afternoon you've carved out for yourselves? Consistency is the hobgoblin of little minds, you propane-burning blockhead. Go ahead and drop a piece of barbecue onto your khakis once in a while. They're only clothes. What do you want, to wear it like new until you die with a full wardrobe? Not me. I'm getting out of this world with a comfy bathrobe, one good eye, and barbecue stuck between my teeth.

Take care of my dog for me.

As far as these men are concerned, their children's paternity is confirmed by matching shirts. →

THE VEIN OF TRAIN WHO'S THAT YOU'RE CALLING A POT BOILER?

If there's two things kids love, it's trains and fire. That's why a kid's dream job is to shovel coal onto a steam engine across the great plains. Too bad, there are no more steam engines, and the closest we'll ever get is a sensible pile of coal in our barbecue. Among our number, though, is a dreamer who refused to bend to the burden of reality. If life hands you lemons, make lemonade, and save some of it to flavor your chicken in your kick-ass new train barbecue. Toot-toot! All aboard the tank engine to Awesometown!

HERE'S POINTING AT YOU, KID

Naturally someone took the great train idea and decided to run in a direction dripping with testosterone, which is not as good a baste as it might sound, unless you're eating testes, which I'm told farm-folk like to do. But not you. Nah, you're a hunter-gatherer, so you nod politely at this pistol-barrel smoker and don't point out the grill proper ruins the effect. After all, the chef might have a gun. See that star on the gaudy burnished steel grip? You're courting the ire someone who loves flash and firearms as much as normal folk love barbecue. Someone who doesn't realize that not all good things combine well.

How American can something get before it's officially Texas?

OPPORTUNITY KNOCKS WORST
EXTREME BRATWURST CHALLENGES

Not everywhere and everywhen is an appropriate barbecue juncture. An example of a time not to barbecue would be on the altar at your wedding, if the bride is vegetarian. After all, it is her day. But you're a sharp lad, you'll land a girl from one of those hilarious neo-pagan religions that pretend to be oppressed and who grill burnt offerings to Cernunnos as part of their wedding rite. Make a wreath of some green willow branches and celebrate your life! Here are some other bad choices.

Oh, sure, it's hard to find a nice backyard in New York, and a man takes what he wants, so you might think this man commands your respect. After all, the barriers are up; he's not blocking traffic. So what's the problem? The problem is this man is not a New Yorker, or he'd know better than to stop in the middle of a walkway. Those damned tourists never know what they're doing. They're always underfoot, and their burgers are dry.

Then we have a fellow closing out the day with some hot food and cool toes. But look again— it's late evening in summer, meaning the tide is likely coming in. If he's not prepared, he's going to have to rush the meat, and that's just unforgivable. I know all the world respects barbecue, but it's equally true that time and tide wait for no man, and he's got both working against him here.

Fun fact: These two pictures are of the same man! From one angle, he looks like a male model in the city. But seen from the left, and with lower lighting, he turns out to be a friendly codger enjoying the surf. Don't tell anyone I let you in on that publisher's trick or it's my head.

I WANT THIS MAN'S LIFE
YES, EVEN HIS SANDALS

When is a grill not a grill? When it's a broiler. Man, that is the life: classic car, lovely home someplace tropical, well-behaved son, and check out the rear end of that luscious vehicle supporting the equally luscious rear end of a hot wife.

This guy is so cool he must have gotten rich illegally.

OINK, OINK PIGS ARE CANNIBALS, BECAUSE EVEN PORK KNOWS HOW GOOD PORK TASTES

These people had a perfectly functional smoker, but they went the extra mile, and that warms my heart. Then they did a lap around that and gave the pig a blackboard on which to pontificate. After all, the food ended up in the grill's stomach before anyone else's, so why shouldn't it be able to opine on the state of today's meal?

CHOP SLAPPING FUN

You see, you have to make barbecue your own. This is a cuter device than I'd want to own, but I'm very glad it exists and that its owner is a curvaceous brunette who tells me I'm welcome to her picnics anytime, sustains eye contact a little too long, then lets her gaze drop in an embarrassment that's purely for show…woah! Sorry. Got a little away from myself there. What I should have been fantasizing about is the chops that you're going to pull out of this bad boy. Flirtatious dames are everywhere, but pork that knows it was cooked in pork is going to try its hardest to please you now that it's learned to fear your top-to-bottom pig stance.

Too bad the portions don't get their own, even tinier blackboard, because it would probably say something like "Don't hurt me! I'll do what you want!" and maybe, "By the way, brunette, Brendan gives great back rubs. Just saying."

Thanks, Pork! You're an ace wingman. I'm sorry to have to eat you now. But not much.

LITTLE GUY DELUXE AND HIS SEDUCTION MACHINE

Little Guy DeLuxe was a brilliant 17th-century inventor and Court Dwarf who eventually rose to command a barony with fortunes earned from the sale of mass-produced replicas of his home. Although originally collector's items among the nobility and never utilized, they became popular with the laboring classes for preventing death by exposure.

The trailers remain popular to this day. Compressing an entire household into a trailer is a genius idea for the bachelor who occasionally needs to pretend to have a family for the weekend. You've got tea, you've got the smallest grill I've ever seen, and you've got a child's bed that is presumably heated by the grill and the steam from the tea. Ooh! Don't forget the air holes! That was a close one.

A MAN OF MYSTERY

It's also useful for dating a divorcee. Simply pop the child into the trailer with a handheld video game and a bag of chips, and enjoy your wall-to-wall sexcapades in the now-private apartment. I'd caution you to carry a spare license plate, though. The whole idea is for her to not find out where your apartment is, and you want to avoid any identifying signifiers. That's why I usually rotate fake tattoos around my body, so if called to paternity suit, I can say, "Plainly, your honor, the dirty word inscribed upon my most private parts begins with the letter F, and therefore cannot be the medieval insult described by the plaintiff. However, if it pleases the court, I will ponder the idea of a redhead in heels and little else long enough to establish this without a doubt."

And that's why my cases get a full article in the NY Post whereas yours are reduced to a brief line in the police logs about drunkenly attempting to ride the giraffes at the zoo.

Wait...how long was I in police custody? Two weeks? Dear Lord, the child is still confined to the trailer!

Hey, look how cleverly we obscured the number plate to protect its owner's privacy! If you were wondering, the license is HMS-PINA4.

HOME ON THE RANGE LET'S STEAL GRANDMA'S STOVE AND GET GRILLING!

Admire here the stove and oven from before electricity existed anywhere other than rainstorms, petting a cat, and staring into my eyes—I'm talking to you, now, ladies. Yes, it seems around '54 or so, the wife had to have wires just because our next-door neighbors 500 wagon wheels down the road got some. Then came the plumbing, and the heat that actually worked, and soon you find yourself dragging this relic of a nobler, cozier era quite literally out to pasture and finally repurposing it into the summer grill.

THE OLD AND GRACEFUL LIFE

That's not what I call gratitude, is it? This thing kept your grandparents alive in the winter. And here's you, wearing a wristwatch that keeps its own time like you're Johnny Too Bad. What happened to your pocketwatch and fob? And your ascot? And your wainscot? And those Scots? All gone. Think of them, won't you, as you tend to this ceramic beast in your backyard? They are but ghosts within its frame, which will teach you a hard lesson about burning everything you think is outdated. I don't want

to sound ignorant, but do they even still have a Scotland, or did they burn the last of it in the '80s? Someone should check, but who wants to travel that far north? It wouldn't be civilized, which brings us back to this stove. Like us, no one wants it because it doesn't fit their comfortable idea of modernity. But you know what else modernity gave us? Nuclear war! And when that idea has had its day, the only ones left will be those of us with these stoves. We'll crawl inside and stay comfortably insulated from heat and radiation, living off grease scrapings until such time as our albino, eyeless Morlock descendants crawl from its husk to reclaim the Earth.

Oh, just think what a barbecue they'll throw!

Of course, your giant cutlery is much harder to come by these days.

WHATEVER ROASTS YOUR BOAT
GETTING TENDER OVER A MOIST HEAT

The floating grill, while a more complicated and risky endeavour, carries a higher reward. There you are, floating on a banana boat with dozens of scantily clad teenage girls (it's okay —you're a teenager too), and the man who sired you now serves you smoked meats like the lowest servant. Truly, you were right to coronate yourself the Palm Frond King of Oahu.

But what's this? Your hubris has attracted the attention of Ku, possessor of powers! Oh, mighty is his wrath, and the curse upon you shall never be lifted till those fair maidens are cast into his volcano (gods like barbecue as much as you or I). Nowhere is safe! For the food, I mean. You yourself are safe, but that barbecue is going is going into the drink if you don't appease the tiki right quick.

THE FISH BITE BACK

Then again, maybe you're not safe. Barbecue is a slow and juicy process, with lots of run-off. You can't dangle your toes in the water next to a smoldering pork carcass and then act surprised when your outing proves shark-bait.

And by the way, it's not like fish ever encounter fire, so don't expect those two-ton stomachs from the deep to flee your smoke the way a wolf might. You know how in lean times, a bear or a lion is made bold by hunger? Hunger is every minute of a shark's life. What were you thinking, bringing children out here to die? All for what? Some smoked pineapple? Mmmm, damn, that's good.

A seafaring society based on hot coals atop pressurized rubber quickly dominates lesser cultures, but is ultimately doomed.

Wow, here are the same kids five years later! Now their innocent game of Marco Polo has taken on adult overtones, as two lads blindly grope the surf for the alpha female. Whosoever—unseeing and drunk—can find her on her rubber doughnut throne, is truly her soulmate, or at least the most evolutionarily viable partner.

IN THE EVENT OF AN EMERGENCY, YOUR MARSHMALLOW DOUBLES AS A FLOTATION DEVICE

You have to wonder if there aren't 220 seats inside, each one with a little kebab perched on it. I'm not saying it wouldn't be delicious, just demented. This barbecue is the only airline whose success rate depends on its contents meeting a fiery end. The only problem with this grill is when it's overcast, the chef cancels dinner just to be cautious. That and there's a two-hour layover between dinner and dessert.

Looking at this, I'd be willing to bet there's a scale version of the *Starship Enterprise* somewhere being used to cook crêpes.

There are two possibilities in this picture. The first is that someone built a scale replica of a Continental jet around his barbecue, and that's disturbing. The second is that Continental commissioned this for their company barbecue, which is much more comforting, until they're no longer flying this class of plane, at which point it gets tossed with not 50 flights under its wing. After all, how many corporate picnics can you throw in a year? All told, something is out of balance here, but let's hope it's not the plane itself. Not only would that endanger the lives of all aboard, it would ruin the cooking process.

This grill breaks the Laws of geometry by folding in half more than seven times.

THE ECONOMY IS EVERYTHING
BUT THERE'S STILL ROOM FOR CONDIMENTS

I don't mind telling you, that grill is a thing of beauty. The whole shindig probably weighs three pounds, or whatever that is in kilogrameters. It's flat, clean, and precise, folds up nicely, doesn't shine too much (so you only have to clean it when it gets greasy), and someone thought to toast the buns ever so slightly. It's too bad those weenies are about 90 days old. I'd rather eat the Styrofoam rocks in the background with the fabric grass for garnish.

TAKE OFF THE HEAT

The artificiality isn't the point here though—it's the loveliness of the setup. This grill doesn't let you get too crazy or fancy, it's just enough for a spur of the moment outing. Burgers and dogs are your options, and you'd better like tomato sauce and mustard, or, chili and mayo, because that handy little tray is your one shot at accessorizing. Wash the whole thing down with the gas station's finest non-brand drink (flavors are red and pine), and just kick back by the mural of the lake.

Yessiree, that is the life, and it's all thanks to this wonderful grill, which folds up flat to fit in the trunk of even the tiniest vehicle. You could strap it to your bicycle if you so felt the inclination, but I have to warn you that's a great way to get burned riding home.

"Throw out the coals, young man," advised the artificial old man sitting in the fake rocking chair on the façade porch, but even though his country wisdom was 100 per cent genuine, my Pop taught me never to waste coals. The scar tissue will only make me more invincible in a fight, and riding my bike saved petrol.

Dad also taught me never to call gas "petrol", but let's not dicker over semantics right now. We've had a lovely afternoon.

REBEL WITHOUT A CAR GRILL WITHOUT A HOPE

Not like I wouldn't be proud to own this, but now that I've seen the two-parter that comes with a good woman who stands by you through thick and thin and bears strong children (she's calling me from page 32), and p.s. is a cooler car...I just don't know what dream to draum. The only way we're going to settle this one is to play a game of chicken at the cliff. Go, Greased Lightning!

Of course, the way I barbecue it's all grease, and there's usually lightning. You're probably not cool enough to attend, but I'll vouch for you to the ladies. Just stay away from my girl, see? Tall and lean, she is, with a coltish pair of gams, and hair as red as the blood seeping from your burger. Sorry, let me cook that a little more for you.

This grill would lose in a race to the fancy blue one on page 32 is my point, assuming they could drive, which they can't. I couldn't tell you who makes a better burger until I've tried them both. This is also true of the wives, the pools, and the dot-com jobs that put you in such affluent if not wholly tasteful surroundings. That's not a criticism by the way. Everyone needs one or two kitsch objects in their house just to remember life is goofy. That's why I backed my car through the wall of my house. Now I have an unorthodox grill not unlike this, and when my friends come over, I can point to the unrepaired damage of what was once a retaining wall and say in my most grating voice, "Women drivers — AM I RIGHT?"

This is why I'm going to die single. Probably of cholesterol next year.

NATURAL BORN GRILLERS WITH FLOWERS ON THE SIDE

I don't know what's going on here. That building can house, at most, five people, but more than a dozen will be fed, according to the grill. Not that I blame them all for moving there. Look at this paradise. It's the reason sentimental country music exists.

OBSESSION MAD ABOUT THE GRILL

Pay no attention to these Packers fans. They're just cheering because the football season ended yesterday, meaning there are only 35 weeks left before the start of the next season.

Focus your attention instead on that beauty of a grill. Sleek yet demure, smoky yet self-contained, she's everything you want in a grill or girl (the words are derived from the same Indo-European root noun, which is unsuitable for reproduction here). The difference is women are not objects, which is what I'd like to take a moment to talk about.

OH, HI DARLING!

You know, we like to have a lot of fun around here at the barbecue fortress, indulging in the lazy joys of food and drink, but there's no finer appreciation in life than the love of a good woman, which must be earned every day. Keep that in mind and assume every sexist joke within these pages is secretly laughing at people who hold such attitudes, or else my girlfriend will kill me. A woman is not a piece of meat, even if she does appreciate a good massage with scented oils. Nor is she a grill, even if both can cook a perfect steak. She is

a person—probably a better one than you. In truth, these men would give up barbecue forever to win the love of a strong woman who makes them the best men they could be. Or alternatively, a weekend with a lingerie model. The male lack of standards isn't the point.

Respect women always, venerate them when they deserve it, and find one who loves football.

My guess is for smoke, they're using a combination of hickory chips and cigars. There will be a special compartment in the bottom three inches of the rig for a tiny man to lie flat and smoke the cigar.

THE WAY WE WERE

In the '50s, the cutting-edge grills ran on enriched uranium: cheap, clean, and almost too efficient. The model pictured here irradiates all meat in a 50ft area. Say! Don't stand so close, Mr. and Mrs. America!

Barbecue at a whim was a rich man's privilege, and many limousines had such a device to feed the upper class on their way to meetings where they conspired to suppress the poor. In-car barbecue fell out of vogue after the single jar of Grey Poupon mustard shared by the highway's aristocrats ran dry.

52
53

Speaking of class warfare, that servile fellow looks almost too happy to be grilling in the hot sun whilst clad in formal wear. If I were Johnny Millionaire over there, I'd be suspicious of my meal. I also wouldn't hold my cigarette over my girlfriend's head, but maybe that's what she pays him for.

BITING OFF MORE IDEA THAN YOU CAN CHEW HEY, CHIP?

A word of caution to those of you thinking about smashing your car into the garage and then stripping it down to a functional grill. Choose your auto carefully. Obviously, you want a vehicle that's no good to anyone, like a DeLorean after 1989, or a Dodge Neon ever. But you also want it to look good, and that's in direct opposition to slicing a car in half and pasting it to your wall. Where are you going to find a perfectly intact Mustang with its guts beyond repair? In all likelihood, you'll end up sticking a pink and yellow polka-dot truck in your garage.

GLOBAL WARMING

And then what? The average grill is a square foot, and it takes a third of a bag of coals. You ever try to heat up seven square feet of truck even if the depth is the same? They'll name cancers after you for all the carcinogens you're burning. And not the fun kind of cancer, either, where you get all the ice cream you can eat, and sponge baths from a sexy nurse. Or was that a tonsillectomy? Either way, you won't be enjoying barbecue.

Don't make this boy's mistake, or you'll end up in some hippie ride in the middle of nowhere. Model yourself after that winner on page 32. He abbreviated the length of the grill after picking a nice model and color, and now he lives in a mansion working 12 hours a week (nine of which are making love to his wife). Play your cards right, and a winner is you!

Alright, Chip, I'll grant you, yes, those sausages look delici—is that my duck apron?

DAVY JONES'S MEAT LOCKER
YOU'VE NEVER BEEN THIS FRESH BEFORE

You can picture it, right? Breaching the surface in slow-motion, its lips peel back to reveal row upon awful row of teeth, ink-black eyes unused to so much light. And you, your spatula in hand, frozen and helpless but to watch as "snap!" go the jaws. The boat lists momentarily with the sudden weight, and you feel yourself stumbling off-balance towards the rail below you. Then the grill, a typical number found at parks around the world, peels off the boat with the groaning wrench of metal bolts, a massive, killer weight momentarily hooked on your vessel but now returned to the sea with a massive belly not nearly full of Ortesanita sausages, quality since 1741.

You can write the whole thing off not as the one that got away, but as the one that got away with your lunch. Catch and release, old son. Catch and release.

Now let's go camping next week and try the same thing again to nab a land-shark.

On a boat, space is at a premium, and on a wooden boat that's probably got more oil and wax per square inch in its planks than the human ear, you don't want a whole lot of sizzle and drizzle. Better to hang those coals over the sea and pray your camera's handy the day a great white shark leaps eight feet out of the water to steal your dinner in one terrific chomp.

03 FLAME-GRILL HEROES

Barbecue, like martial arts, developed everywhere in a variety of styles. Different times call for different men, and the stalwart grillmeister heeds his destiny without regard to secondary, earthly affairs like paying rent or acknowledging his offspring. Here are some of these legendary heroes in action and apron.

FIRE MEN LAUGHING IN THE FACE OF DANGER

These lords of the flame revel in a skin-searing kiss from the passionate coals. That shaved second of ignition contains the mysteries of life. Raw energy compels itself skyward to announce the triumphant discovery of fire! In this fleeting moment, a man is truly a man, hurling himself back from the untamable power he has birthed. Gone before it can be fully subsumed into our triumphant flesh, the blazing burst recollects our own inception, when spark became inferno. For a second, we are young again.

Also, a porkpie hat is a lovely accessory here, owing to its sharp, square design that really lets the scalp breathe on a hot summer's eve.

Proper caution is exercised in this case by practiced grillers, each of whom attempts to fling his two friends in danger's path as offering to fire's unquenchable hunger for human sacrifice. Cleats are necessary at such a gathering, as is mango salsa. To prepare mango salsa, buy three dozen mangoes, four bell peppers, six red onions, one bunch of cilantro, and hand them all to your wife, because you don't make any dish that isn't a threat to your life.

NOW FOR THE FUN PART

In a classic case of too many cooks, these firelords appear to have already prepared the sausages to the right of the image, and are now lighting a separate batch of coals for fun and death-defying stunts. Such wastefulness, while attractive to the opposite sex (women, if you were wondering), is disrespectful of coal, and taunts the ancient fire gods to claim their due.

Always keep a spare lamb around to throw on any unexpected hot grills that arise at your party.

People you don't want to barbecue with...

...and a person you do.

IN THE COMPANY OF MONSTERS
PUT DOWN THAT DRINK, AND WALK ON BY

It's all too perfect, isn't it? Oh, I know it looks tempting, with the challenging glare of those icy rich ladies who so plainly do not love their self-obsessed boyfriends—and in fact, cannot love anyone for so long as they clutch the inhumane values of their class. The manly instinct is to drink this party's beer, seduce its women, and be gone before the first round of croquet. But you are better than this, and not even those perfectly grilled meats can settle your inner dæmon, who knows by the prickling hairs on your arm that something isn't right here.

Maybe it's a confidence scheme. Maybe it's a swingers' party. Maybe the blonde used to be a man. Perhaps you even question the hot pink paint upon the bungalow walls. One thing's for sure. You need to politely and presently walk away, because this is the first act of a horror movie.

THANKFULLY, THERE'S HOPE
You can have all of these delights without selling your soul. Look at our friend on the right, relaxing in a hammock on a pleasant day, as a dame who's ten kinds of 10 thoughtfully tends to his need. No doubt this modern man will reciprocate by cooking, cleaning, and sleeping in the wet spot tonight. Because he's class.

The only thing missing from this otherwise-idyllic moment is a labrador retriever with a cold nose to balance the beer atop.

THE CLASSIC HONEST TO GOODNESS!

Bobby always remembered that day with the Petersons. Mr. Peterson, fresh from the golf course, had expertly steered the family station wagon to the local park, where Mrs. Peterson produced a thermos of sweet, homemade lemonade. The children and Skip, the yellow Labrador retriever, played by the pond's edge. As they caught frogs and let them go, Bobby noticed the way Susie's braid swung in the sunlight and glinted with hidden traces of gold. Bobby closed his eyes and let the sun warm his skin. When he could hold on to that perfect moment no longer, he exhaled, and joined his friends at the table.

Expertly seared beer brats sizzled on the grill, sweating hot juices. "Try some of this gourmet mustard, Bobby," said Mr. Peterson proudly. "It really brings out the taste." Bobby trepidly ladled some onto his bun. When he looked up, Mrs. Peterson was smiling at him. "Have more if you want," her voice chimed. Bobby realized then that Danny's mom and dad were not at all like his own.

YEARS LATER

After his parents' divorce, after his older brother came back from Vietnam, after two women had loved him and then not, Bobby thought back to those days. His hair was newly clipped at Mr. Benigni's barbershop, the baseball was about to sock satisfyingly into his mitt, and his body soared through the air above the field, free from gravity for an infinite moment.

It was in a thrift store down in Greenwich Village that Bobby saw the portable grill, its plaid case scuffed and rubbed thin. He knew it could not be the same one the Petersons had owned, but still…The firetruck-red base beamed proudly at him. *Yes*, it promised, *There is still time.*

Two days later found him on the roof of his Lower East Side apartment building, practicing the art of barbecue, and dressed against the fall cold.

Life isn't perfect, but a day can be.

LOVE IN THE SUBURBS
SMOLDERING FIRE

You can't force a day to be pleasant with your spring garb.

This couple doesn't have much, but they have each other. A scant pitcher of red drink, doubtlessly cut with vodka, divides their lazy Sunday in twain. Having already made love with the morning sun piercing blinds drawn to keep out the rumble and roar from the highway outside their window, they now don whatever clothes are not in the wash and step outside.

Tim sears the cheapest cut of steak to be had as Gillian gazes toward a horizon devoid of promise. Tomorrow a letter will arrive from the university, informing her that her transcript will be closed if she does not send in payment for the autumn semester. She wonders with less hesitation than yesterday whether to inform Tim of her pregnancy. In days of old, consumption of beef was thought to influence the internal humors to produce a male heir.

CHIOICE IS AN ILLUSION

Tim's plans to leave his cubicle job this year will fall forgotten to the side of his duties as an expectant father. Employers will notice his sudden recommitment to work, and reward him with a promotion in December. Additionally, he will become the *de facto* chef at the company picnic, renowned for his ability to wrest exciting flavors from the least portions of meat.

In 20 minutes, the steak will be consumed, and the couple will search the clouds for shapes, imposing meaning on the random gusts of fate.

In 30 minutes, they return inside and make love again, this time with a drunken furor that seals their bond, trusting one another to take selfishly and return it lovingly another day.

In 80 minutes, they collapse, exhausted, upon one another, letting their mingled sweat cool in the spring air.

In 88 minutes, Gillian makes Tim the happiest man in the world.

The next day, the nutrients reach her bloodstream and the future president enjoys her first steak.

SAY, BBQ, YOU'RE THE MOST!
THINGS GET HOT IN THE SUMMER OF LOVE

"Let's see here, we've got watermelon, we've got hot dog rolls, we've got marshmallows for the potato salad, and there's an entire chicken for each of us...Okay, looks like this convoy's ready to roll," mused Skip.

It wasn't the kids' usual custom to enjoy such a wholesome good time, or even to use pots and pans on a high-intensity grill, but that was why they enjoyed a reputation around their sleepy beach town as The Go-Go-Krrrrrazy Gang—the swingin'est, peppiest, ZAZZIEST collaboration of kooks in 1967! Oh brother, just when you think you have a handle on these teens, they're mixing up a shindig from the other side!

SUDDENLY, DOUBT CREEPS IN

"Are we contrarian simply to have something to oppose?" Skip wondered, furrowing his brow. Though he did not yet know it, the serpent was in the garden. Doubt had entered his frame of existence. It was for this reason that he would be the first to leave the gang at the end of summer and take a job in finance. Sarah, or

"Namaste Bliss," as she'd taken to calling herself, held no such speculation as she turned the bird carcasses on the rotisserie. "To think, me of all people, preparing our bird friends for consumption!" she laughed to herself. Her spiritual guru forbade eating meat, but she had seen a burger wrapper in the rubbish when she went to his office to confront him about the growing number of pregnancies in their church, The Temple of the Cosmic Phoenix.

Chuckie and Babs, by contrast, had a lovely time that evening, finished their studies, and celebrated their 39th wedding anniversary watching reruns of I Love Lucy.

Date

Good lord, look at that glow. Are they using coals, or thermite?

GRRRILLERS!

In this early Neo-Classical barbecue, we see the traditional elements that were once stock and staple: the checkerboard apron, chef hat, sandals, and garish yellow house, which all represent man's desire to eat barbecued foods. The sandals are symbolic of fertility and general manliness.

Every solstice, neo-pagans construct traditional dowsing pits. A bag of coal is carried around the countryside until its bearer's arms grow tired. He then constructs a traditional Celtic tripod. Meat is tethered over flame and punched amongst three players to tenderize. Whomever's feet it falls at, eats it. The other two are sacrificed to wild gods.

Bold is the man who grills nude before spattering chicken. Bold, and quite possibly drunk. This activity is great fun, so long as your guests are neither dressed nor mortified. If he survives, he will likely receive a beneficent entendre from a female requesting a hot dog but indicating she already has a bun.

Now that's a man who loves his family, or at least his barbecue. Snow is no deterrent to his desire for grilled meats. Though baked on one side and frozen on the other, at least he'll be chapped all over. This is going much better than his attempted snowball fight last June.

BIG TEX 20 GALLONS OF APPETITE IN 10 GALLONS OF HAT

Big Tex moved up to California when he got too good at his job. After manning the oil pumps for years, they made him a manager, and then a regional coordinator. He pulled crews together with hard work and soft steak, throwing legendary barbecues at the end of a long project. He was a Texas man through and through.

A FISH OUT OF MARINADE

It damned near broke his heart when the company sent him to Los Angeles. But he was a Texan, never saying no to hard work. Always go bigger, was his philosophy. He hadn't found his limits yet.

Big Tex was an oil and gas man, and propane was his method. He could wrangle any chop, slice or slab into sublime salaciousness. "I just don't trust a man," he'd laugh, "what don't take his steak medium rare." Any more than that

was wasteful and subdued. Any less, barbaric. In LA his fellow executives ate *chi-chi* plates of seaweed and tofu that weren't but a forkful. They thought golf was a sport, hired someone else to tend their lawns, and worst of all— they cheered for the Raiders. The goddamn *Raiders*.

He jumped through the ranks like a bullfrog on fire. Before long, they moved him again.

AND LANDED ON THE OTHER SIDE OF THE POND

In Aberdeen, Scotland, Big Tex's new neighbors stared hungrily at his handiwork. The old man had to admit, it was turning out pretty good, considering the unfamiliar cuts of meat here. At least he had appreciative company. It might not have real football, but it was a start.

yessir, things had turned out all right for a hard-working Texas boy. →

THE GUARDIAN OF THE UNIVERSE
SLICE OF OLD-FASHIONED, ANYONE?

Found on every bowling team in the world is a fellow who doesn't say much or stand out in a crowd, but has a tempered passion. He's one of a secret brotherhood that goes about the world, quietly cleaning, adjusting, and tightening it. Society would collapse without these rarely acclaimed maintenance men. Note the perfect height of his lawn, his crisp shirt, and his orderly garbage cans.

He even appears to have converted some old junk into a smokehouse. Why? Because he knows barbecue done right. He won't grill the best food you've ever tasted, but he'll never, ever make a bad meal in his life. He knows the book and he sticks to it.

It's not that it would perturb him to deviate. Life is chaotic, and he takes that in his stride. He would happily try your papaya glaze…at your barbecue. His own satisfaction, however, lies in Things Done the Proper Way.

THE STEADY LESSONS OF 5,000 GENERATIONS
In your ragtag World War II commando squad, he'd be the munitions expert, and all his equipment would be clean and well-oiled. He'd keep his head in any circumstance, and quietly stop internal strife when it became counterproductive to morale.

Such a man would never read this barbecue book—indeed, would not own any book of barbecue at all. But if he did, it would be one slim volume, with no more than a dozen recipes, and primarily devoted to proper use and care of the kit.

We salute you, Mr. Temperance. Your essential work has been appreciated.

MORE GRRRILLERS!

The distinctive pattern and cut of this specimen's undergarment indicate he is British. The three dozen sausages under his care suggest he is part of a much larger herd, while the goofy hat is typical of a polyamorous society in which members need not display impressive qualities to mate. Goddamn modern hippies.

In American society, isolated males rule over small territories. Consuming four burgers at once is not uncommon, as the flabby physique presents a formidable bulk which may be mistaken for power. Note the bright yellow piping on the shorts, a sign that this specimen is not yet mature enough to mate.

Transcendental marination empowers this guru to levitate off the coast of Greece. The practice was common for centuries, but is dying out due to processed, store-bought marinades. Close examination of the photograph suggests the kebab meat is either human or Pegasus. The plastic jars contain humanity's ills and must never be opened.

Dad built the brick grill a couple of years after he and mom were married. I was eight, and helped by stirring the mortar. This picture was taken before we found out he had three other families elsewhere in Suffolk County. We had a tournament to see who got the rights to him.

BACKYARD EDISON EXPLORING THE UNIVERSE ONE BITE AT A TIME

For some people, the universe is a puzzle to be solved. These are the pioneers who discover cheat codes in video games and abandon plans for a helicopter to paint the Mona Lisa. They turn oil barrels into racecars, lemon juice into cleaning agents, and expensive computers into expensive computers spread across the room. They never get so emotionally attached that they wouldn't slice their dearest possessions open, rip out their guts, and solder them into new shapes to launch themselves at the moon. With one exception: the tools themselves are inviolate.

WE WHO ARE ABOUT TO FRY, SALUTE YOU

So here's to the hackers, crackers, freakers, and tweakers! The people who build a flamethrower at home, not because grills are impossible to light but because *What will happen if we do?* People who plunge elbow deep into the dirt of life! They're the ones who put rub on barbecue to see if the meat lasts longer, who marinate and brine, inject and baste to keep it tender, who learn the melting points of sugars and the boiling points of oils.

You'll find them everywhere in the rural areas, having had to disassemble, reconfigure, and make the most of equipment from an early age. You'll find them blasting huge belches of fire at a dry, wooden stage, not because it's wise, but because it's *clever*.

You'll find them in the hospital ward, eyeballing their IV drip and wondering how to bypass the regulatory dispensation, not because they want to overdose, but because they want to construct a fireproof version for their 12-hour pig roast.

78
79

Attack life. Try new things! Make a device that connects square pegs to round holes. Move things around until they work for you. But for God's sake, obtain ample health coverage first.

BBQ QUIZ SECRETS OF THE BACK YARD

Can you find 15 things wrong with this picture and one thing absolutely right? Give yourself two minutes, or whatever the metric equivalent of a minute is.

While you're thinking about it, here's a hint: the chef looks like his clothing was selected for him by a foreign child. Not that we have anything against foreigners, you understand, simply against children.

Also, this isn't one of the answers, but check out that guy in the background. Is he about to trample the garden? Because he's half-off the patio right now and he looks to be pondering the idea.

...OKAY, LET'S SEE HOW YOU DID!

1. The conical shape of the grill, while excellent for concentrating heat and lighting a fire, wastes coals that would be better spent evenly cooking the meat.
2. There is no tasteful shrine to preceding grillmeisters at the helm of the cook station.
3. The gentleman is wearing raised dark socks with shorts, but is not yet senile.
4. The wife is not scolding her husband.
5. The raw burger patties are too small, unless making sliders, but since both parties are sober enough to stand up, they can't possibly be having sliders.
6. The children—dear God, where are the children?!
7. Oh, they went to play at Tommy's house. He has that new Playstation game. That's alright, then.
8. What? On a lovely day like today? I disapprove of children indoors where they can vex their betters.
9. I already told them they could. Don't undermine my authority in front of them!
10. I'm sorry, Lucy, this marriage no longer works. It's all gone wrong, all of it!
11. Is this because I spurned your advances this morning?
12. ...Yes.
13. Tch! Silly bugger. I was just hungover.
14. Oh, is that all? But of course! I quite forgot it was Wednesday!
15. Come here, you.
16. Not now, dear. The burgers are very nearly ready.

And they all ate happily ever after.

KEEP IT SIMPLE A LITTLE BIT OF POOLSIDE HEAVEN

Sometimes, the job doesn't want a big project. A bad artist can only do simple things. A good artist can do complex ones. A great artist does complexity in a simple way. And a master knows when pure simplicity is all you need.

Case in point: poolside on vacation. It's lunch, and you're going someplace nice for dinner. There's no need to go crazy here. Heat up the grill, grab some dogs and burgers, a few basic condiments, and relax with a beer. Tell the kids not to run or they'll crack their heads open.

IGNORANCE IS BLISS. FATTENING, TASTY BLISS

It's your vacation, friend. Save the laborious undertaking for the pig roast for your final night in paradise. You don't want to fill up, anyway. You intend to jump in the pool and splash around with your family. This is the last vacation before they start driving or dating, so enjoy those moments with one fewer thing to worry about. Let the gut get a little bigger for a week. You can work out when you get back. That's why this guy's an alright type.

He doesn't need anyone to tell him all that. What more could he possibly want in this sunny hour? Besides a passionate kiss on the sly from his wife, nothing. It's been a good day, and there are better things to come. Now is the time to enjoy their anticipation.

The simple life, brother, that's what it's all about. Just remember to save a dog and a beer for us. We'll be there soon.

04 GETTING PSYCHED AND PREPPED

Too far, young man. It's one thing to wake up drunk in Mexico next to an untethered stove. It's quite another to wake up next to a stove that has been rendered non-functional.

This is the point where many books instruct you in the proper methods of barbecue and safety. Go read one of those before you do any cooking. Personally, I learned everything I know about cooking at Clown College, or I would have if I had been accepted there. Instead, I settled for University College Dublin.

Nevertheless, there are important questions to ask oneself, like "Do I use a rub or a marinade?"—"Are my knives clean and sharp?" and "Do I spend enough time with my kids?" Pursuant to that, "Why does my son look like my neighbor?" Now you see why it's good to keep your knives sharp.

HOW TO LOOK GOOD IN SOOT
OLD KING COAL

Charcoal is my preferred method of cooking. The coals give the food a wonderful, smoky flavor, and it instantly dirties one's hands to provide a façade of hard work. In the north of England, they bake a coal into a herring dish, and whoever finds it in their serving is doomed to be married that year. Starry-gazey pie, they call it, with the fish heads a'flopping all about.

Charcoal is notoriously difficult to light, with each piece too infuriatingly inert for use as kindling. Most people soak their coals in phenol-based lighter fluid, but others feel the imparted chemical taste interferes with the otherwise delicious carcinogens.

IF YOU MUST BE CAREFUL, SO BE IT

A cautionary word: it's stupid and dangerous to add accelerants to already hot coals, which is why I often do it. That doesn't mean you should make my mistakes. I've used cooking oil when I've run out of lighter fluid. Does that sound wise? No, clearly not.

Once your coals are hot and grey and without open flame, spread them out in a single layer throughout or cluster at one end if you intend to grill indirectly. Set one aside to cool for your children's stocking. When you're done cooking, close the grill and any vents. The fire will asphyxiate, and you can save the ashes for a comely, virtuous maiden to sweep up until she's rescued by a handsome prince with a glass slipper. Sounds crazy, I know, but these things happen. Never to me, though. (*sigh*)

A typical American football fan sets the world on fire without regard for any definition of taste.

Make no mistake: the flame is not your friend. This is an alliance of convenience, and if you give fire any wiggle room in your terms, it will seize it.

A 2,000-year-old tree that thought it was smart gets what's coming to it. That'll teach it to exist where man can see it!

WOODEN YOU KNOW WHACK!

Cooking with wood is a direct path to our caveman roots, but an even more direct path to our caveman limbs, branches, and twigs. Mere briquettes are not enough for you. Trees must fall, that they might not purify the air and prevent the aromatic smoke of your achievements from tempting the gods themselves!

BESTIR YOURSELF

First, select a very dry piece of wood. I recommend cinema's Roger Moore, but oak will do. Ash is also good, I assume, because it's called ash. Then simply make a fire. I'm afraid I don't know the recipe, but it involves the application of high heat to materials with low burning point. Perhaps if you rub your knees together while wearing corduroy trousers?

There are fellows who will start you a fire for the right price, but that's more of an insurance matter. For most cooking, your flame should remain in a single area of about two feet, so you want to leave the gas in the car and use traditional methods for generating a fire. Try rubbing two sticks together until you're exhausted and

Like the moments of self-realization following a one-night stand, this man considers how he has used nature without regard for its well-being.

devoid of hope. If you can't find any sticks, casually discard a cigarette while starring in a public service advertisement. Whatever your approach, do not summon the fire department; it turns out they are rather anti-fire.

Finally, remember to plant two trees for every one that you burn. Put them very close together and watch them fight over a period of years. Which one submits? The loser is weak, and will become your next bonfire. It's nature's way.

PROPANE THE GAS THAT MAKES BARBECUING EASY...TOO EASY

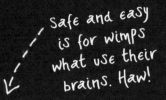

Safe and easy is for wimps what use their brains. Haw!

The advantages of propane are temperature control, odorless cooking, a drip pan, and instant lighting. The disadvantage is snide jokes from other men. Despite being the only cooking method that can blow you up even when you're not using it, propane doesn't garner respect. Oh well! Next method.

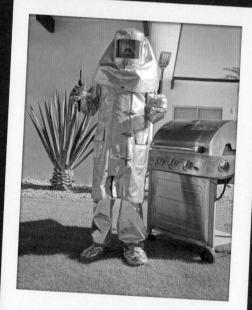

Although a flammable gas, propane is safer than you'd think.

What wood lacks in control, it more than makes up in satisfaction.

SMOKING NOW FOR ADULTS TOO!

Smoke is what gives barbecue its flavor, which is why the smoking section is the most desirable seating in any restaurant.

If you're not cooking over a log, you'll want to use wood chips. The reason is the smoke flavors the meat, and that flavor differs according to the type of wood you use. Certain woods are complementary to specific meats. For example, chicken or pork benefit from mesquite chips, whereas nymph and sprite are perfect for that enchanted faerie wood they made the wardrobe out of in *The Chronicles of Narnia*. Any decent grocer's in a hobbit neighborhood should have magic rings.

If you live in a science-fiction future without trees, you may substitute a tree-pill.

MUCH SMOKE, BUT NO MIRRORS

Soak the wood chips in water, though you can also use apple juice, beer, or wine, all of which confer the advantage of costing more while changing almost nothing. By throwing money at useless crap, you'll make a perfect façade of a rich man's tendency to show off his wealth. Everyone around you will assume you to be upper-crust, and do whatever they can to

FWOOM!

garner your favor. But whatever moisture you decide to use, rest assured that its convection will create the essential "acid rain" taste your meat may otherwise lack.

To use, throw the chips onto the coals. Yes, it's really that easy, unless you're one of those propaney bastards I warned you not to become. You can also improvise one with any container that has a couple of openings to release the smoke slowly and steadily. Just don't light the chips on fire is all I'm saying.

LIGHTING THE BARBIE HOW TO SINGE FRIENDS & IMMOLATE PEOPLE

Depending on the type of grill, you'll either have it lit in seconds, or you have something other than propane. Congratulations on selecting the hard-fought path to glory, old son! Try not to starve to death before winter comes. Those of you who survive, we'll meet you back here for chapter five.

PROPANE

Propane's simplicity is the secret to its popularity. Open the valve atop the tank, turn on the flame controls, and press the starter button. Then run like hell.

Simplicity is also key to propane's lack of respect. Come, let us leave behind these fools with their quick and easy methods, and—like Prometheus—bring forth fire from nothing.

After all, that went so well for him.

A chimney starter makes lighting so easy, it's legally considered propane.

Where are the women at this barbecue? And what's...what's that strange cut of meat?...Good lord!

Even bears will feel drawn to admire your magnificent handiwork.

TRY THIS! Add a beefy flavor to your coal by rubbing a steak on it. Then eat the coal. Ha ha! Some guys'll fall for anything.

The lungs are nature's bellows, and should be used to agitate tepid coals. Inhale a wide gust, and puff an oxygen-rich blast into the heart of the beast.

CHARCOAL

Pile coals loosely enough for air to flow throughout. You don't want to suffocate the flame. Treat charcoal like a baby: brag unbearably to your friends, then fob it off on an *au pair*.

For those of us who can't afford to exploit immigrants, our coal merely smolders and our children grow up well-rounded people who enjoy our love and attention. Fortunately, something can be done about the former. That something is called a chimney starter.

This nifty device traps heat, forcing it up through the coals with no need for lighter fluid! Don't be fooled by the handle; these things are impossible to pick up without an oven mitt.

Whichever your method, throw a match into the briquettes. Then run like hell.

WOOD

Arrange kindling that lights easily but burns slowly in a pile. I recommend you douse granite rocks in gasoline, but I also seek to console your bereaved widow with a sexy shoulder. You'll probably do fine with dry leaves and pine needles.

Center the kindling beneath logs slightly elevated so the smoke has someplace to escape. It's wise to surround the fire with rocks for containment and to radiate heat back toward the source. Some of the best grills are stone or brick, but these are a challenge to bring to barbecue competitions.

Light the kindling. Then run like hell.

THE RULES A GENTLEMAN'S GUIDE TO PROPER PILLAGING

1 Rub oil on grill racks to prevent grilled foods from sticking; then rub some on your chest to seduce women. This never fails. Make sure your buddies are there to take pictures.

2 Marinate to preserve moisture and add flavor; you don't have to marinate with wine or beer, but why wouldn't you?

3 Add herb branches and orange peels atop the coals to impart an exotic taste to the meat; this is a prehistoric tradition to which you may add a modern flavor by burning computer circuitry. The binary code adds new zip to the meat, and it's a great way to dispose of toxic metals that would otherwise be bad for the environment.

4 Cook fish in a close-knit mesh rack to prevent the meat from breaking apart. If you're sure your companion's not going to sleep with you, I see no reason to put this much effort into cooking for her. Unless… is she rich?

5 Baste with marinade or oil before, during, and after the cooking process. Well…probably after. Definitely during. Maybe before? To be safe, baste everything, everywhere, always.

6 Soak wooden skewers in water an hour before grilling to prevent them from burning. *Fun fact:* even if you swim for an hour before cooking, you yourself will still be vulnerable to flame.

7 Consider pork to be done when no red juices run out of the meat. Consider beef to be done when it stops mooing.

8 Cheat: sear meat in a hot pan, then throw it in a slow-cooker for the day. This is the dirty secret of many barbecue restaurants, and produces tastier ribs than you'll wrest from a grill. Depending where you live, it may be called a crockpot or *Wee Saelly Goob*, because Scottish people never let the English language tame them.

If you're eating anything else, you're really not using your grill to its full potential.

9 Use a clean plate for the cooked meat, and never reuse the plate that you put raw meat on. The reason for this is you don't wish to poison your friends and family. Or is that exactly what you want the police to think?

10 Cook over glowing coals, not roaring fires. This is also the secret to a happy marriage. Radiant heat produces a smoky, moist, succulent entrée. For best results, shove the coals to one side and the meat to the other for indirect heat. Are we still talking about marriage? I have no idea, because my only love in life is barbec—Oh God, she's never coming back, is she?

11 Let the meat sit for ten minutes after cooking. Once you take it off the grill, it continues to cook, so cover it on a dish and let those lovely juices reach a relaxed state. Yes, you've got time for another beer.

This is how a man stationed at a grill pictures himself looking to other people...

...and this is how he actually looks.

05

THE KIT— TOOLS, GLORIOUS TOOLS

I don't want to sound like a know-it-all, but your first problem is everything's gone topside-down.

Grillmeisters love to debate what truly qualifies barbecue, as opposed to just grilled meats. Some say it's the smoke, others the seasoning, and a few the sauce.

In any case, getting the gear is indubitably satisfying, unless you're forced to depend on Christmas gifts from your disillusioned wife. Just remember—once tooled up, you are capable of literally any masterpiece, however glorious or horrific it may be.

PROTECTION HOW TO LOOK DAINTY
BATTLING PRIMAL ELEMENTS IN ARMOR

I also like to dress the chicken in a little tuxedo if I'm grilling indirectly.

Always wear protection. That advice has been co-opted by condom campaigns, but obviously I'm not telling you to wear one of those, because they don't feel as good. No, I mean don padded gear to rebuff hot grease and fire, which, while tolerable, may ruin a ratty t-shirt with ten good years left in it.

You might think it funny to wear a clever apron with some borrowed *non-sequitur* wit like, "You don't have to be crazy to kiss the cook...BUT IT HELPS!" You didn't have to be easily amused, either, but you made your decision. Did you come here to have fun? Fun is for the armed forces. You're here to **barbecue**.

IN WHICH SHARKS ARE MENTIONED YET AGAIN

Be simple and dignified in your choice of apron, as the dainty garment itself unmans you. Personally, I wear a tuxedo when I barbecue. It's a respect thing. To protect my garments from grease, I just turn the cape around. However, not even the most genteel gloves are protection from heat. It's almost like they

have the opposite effect. That's why you should have a good, insulated oven mitt or three. A double-knit oven glove is exceptionally useful, but I prefer a pair of mitts that look like sharks. They go well with the tux. And dude—you're picking things up with shark heads. This used to be the sort of product you could never find, but someone now knits a pair every week on the internet, which is also how I got skull and crossbone cufflinks. Again: tuxedo.

Note the baster, which is a family heirloom made of pig's bladder and hollowed-out mutton bone.

Pictured here: the almost entirely self-sufficient man.
Not pictured: beer, woman (presumed to be taking picture with beer in her hand).

This youngster has been
raised to respect the
traditions of his elders,
and will be rewarded
with bratwurst in Heaven.

GETTING GRABBY
AND FLIPPING OUT

You could flip a steak all day with these, though that would be very rude to the steak

It's not unhygienic to flip the food with your fingers; fire will purify all. It's merely painful and amateurish. Therefore, one requires three simple devices for the manipulation of meats upon the sizzling iron-lattice of our gastronomic altar.

TONGS

Excellent for picking up all manner of sausage, steak, bird limb, and kebab. Use tongs as an extension of your pinchy fingers, and remember they tend to have a very fine grip. Foods of a heavier weight and/or in want of less squeezing may suit the utility of a…

BBQ FORK

This simple, two-tined stabbing device will help you turn heavier weights like ham legs, brisket, whole chickens, and the crippling guilt of not doing enough to save your relationship with The One That Got Away. As it is often important not to pierce the meat, lest its juices run freely like your tears that day love slipped out of your arms forever, you are wise to use a fork in conjunction with the utilitarian…

In his youth, this man could shotgun a beer and crush the can on his skull.

SPATULA

A necessity for flipping burgers, easing fish off the grill, and providing an inherently funny word to toss around. Say it to yourself a few times: spatula, spatula, spatula! It's one of the most satisfying terms in the English language. Use it for foods whose weight and mass are evenly distributed, and which are unlikely to roll indecorously around the grill. When you need to pick up an item of dubious structural integrity, the spatula's your man.

RACKED AND STACKED HOW TO PACK SLACK CRAP IN A BASKET TRAP

Food appreciates a gentle massage before you lay it down by the fire.

Sometimes we're victims of our own success. I, for example, cannot walk these streets without hordes of sexy, violent women chasing me to test my legendary skills as a lover. You, midway through your education, now know how to make succulent entrées but have no idea how you're going to flip all that fall-off-the-bone goodness. That's why you want a rib rack.

What sounds like an early design for a corset is in fact a steel picket or mesh trap to support and press dear meat to fickle bone. Similar devices may be had for kebabs, which love to spill their contents. Such contraptions are at their most useful when grilling fish, an entrée known to slice itself. A basket is essentially the same thing, but, as you might suspect, rather baskety, and useful for smaller nuggets and vegetables.

IN WHICH SHARKS, SURPRISINGLY, ARE NOT MENTIONED

These are all good learning devices for cooks who have developed strength, but not finesse. Basically, people who learned everything they know about lovemaking from pornography. Eventually you'll learn the most important lessons in grilling: how to use a lighter touch, the proper time to turn the meat, and why vegetable kebabs aren't worth your time.

All considered, these devices have got their moments, and some recipes even require such things, but you have to deduct at least 5 points from yourself in normal circumstances. Unless you're using propane, in which case, why are you worried? You have no credit left to lose.

Kebabs, right properly shished. Note the extremely rural setting and the female model—key elements in the scorecard for a perfect barbecue.

everything you've
ever wanted –
a hot chick with
a great rack.

Aliens can often be detected by their calm love of fire and distinct non-resemblance to one another.

FIRE IN THE PIT HOW TO AVOID BLACK HOLES

For their own good, do not feed these to rabbits. Elephants could handle them, though.

So your fire's alight, and you're ready to toss the meat to its enviably hot fate, eh? Not so fast, my good man. Here are a few esoteric products that let you turn up the heat, vary the hot spots, or simply tinker in God's domain (the barbecue pit).

If you ever meet this woman, marry her on the spot. She's lithe, graceful, and cooks a mean bbq.

WOOD PELLETS

Resembling rabbit feed, these sawdust-composite beads are typically used by custom grills as the main heat source, fed slowly and deliberately into the inferno. However, a discerning chef can scatter a small amount amid the coals for use much like wood chips. Remember: a little smoke goes a very long way, but not as far as I went with your sister.

LAVA ROCKS

These little guys spread out like coals in propane grills and cook food evenly. Modern propane tends to be precise, so their use has dropped off. They're very porous and absorb a lot of grease, so watch out for flare-ups. If you're setting up different cooking zones in a charcoal grill, these can be handy in the right spot.

CERAMIC BRIQUETTES

The other thing that killed off lava rocks was the prevalence of ceramic, which sidesteps the grease problem and is easier to come by. Environmental regulations now protect volcanoes from being slaughtered for their lava.

OTHER ACCELERANTS

Let me tell you about the only accelerant you need, the most powerful known to man—LOVE! Love compels a man to feats unimaginable. Love sends the soul streaking across the world with infinite mass. Love warms the coldest heart. It's not very good for cooking, but life will be your feast! Let it propel you into the arms of a good woman, man, or pre-op transsexual.

THE GLORIOUS MOMENT OF INCEPTION

Get that grill going by any means necessary! You're free to light the fire with full prejudice. Under the terms of several non-proliferation treaties, small nuclear devices are permissible if you demonstrate they would favorably flavor the food.

If your uranium is depleted, use charcoal lighter fluid. Stand clear, toss a match, and guard your eyebrows.

2) Cardiovascular degeneration
3) Fireballs again.

whoops! Hydrogen atoms are a great starter, but can be hard to control.

Gas is great for Being Part of the Problem, as well as a superb makeshift incendiary device. It does, however, tinge the meat with the acrid tang of ruthless corporations' ill-gotten wealth. A sweeter version can be had with locally pumped organic gasoline.

BEER HOLDERS GETTING TO GRIPS WITH THE REAL ESSENTIALS

My old man used to say the only beer holder worth carrying was a belly. He later died of liver problems. Thankfully, when I say "my old man," I mean the kook at the local pub, not my father, whose paunch is only mildly distended by age and hernia. The point of this story is that at 98.6°, the human body is a terrible way to keep beer cool. Use a traditional insulated cooler.

The cooler is a marvelous device which separates outside air from inside by a mysterious phantom zone which reacts to neither temperature. It's the only device used in heart transplantation which you are qualified to operate. The original Ark of the Covenant was likely a rudimentary bronze cooler.

AUSTRALIAN GIRLS. WOW.

A handy, lightweight way to keep individual beers cold is a soft, foam sleeve further insulated by a wacky saying. It may lead people to think you're a vacationing Australian, though, so be careful. Don't get me wrong, they're a lovely people, but they celebrate Christmas in the summer. Does that sound right to you?

(Pay my snarky demeanour no mind, Australia. I'm just jealous because your women are gorgeous and your men die in the most interesting animal attacks.)

Cute Australian women have an open invitation to my barbecue.

Insulation is a luxury worry for many of the world's keener grillers.

Pictured: Comfort at home. Not pictured: Class.

Here are some more alternatives for storing or chilling your beer.

- Iceland: Surprisingly affordable in these strenuous economic times.
- Your neighbor's refrigerator: It's common knowledge that full fridges run more efficiently. Do him the kindness of loading up his shelves to streamline energy use.
- Your wife's expression: There's nothing frostier after you ask her to "Fetch me another beer, sweetcheeks." It may arrive at high-velocity, however.
- Hell: It is quite likely that Hell will freeze over before your wife brings you that beer, in which case, problem solved.
- Greenland: Geography's best-kept secret thanks to lying Vikings, this frigid landmass lies about all but unused. However, you are advised to first try Hell, which is more bearable, and home to a slightly greater number of Greenlanders. (Eleven.)

This sort of lackadaisical grill-tending is frankly disturbing.

DAMES THE ONLY THING BETTER THAN BARBECUE

If she offers to help, give her a beer and a chair. You're all about breaking down stereotypes.

Brother, you've got to have dames. The things we love about barbecue are the qualities we love in women—fundamentally sweet with a smoky air, just a touch of saltiness for character, and the hotter the better. Also: breasts.

The fact is, there just ain't nothing like a dame, not even another dame. But maybe two other dames. Say, *there's* an idea…

I'M GETTING A SEXISM HANGOVER

At the heart of it, what satisfies a man about barbecue? Delicious, fatty meat? You're right. But beyond the heart of it—say, the left ventricle—lies this scientific explanation I just now devized without any science whatsoever: man's biological role is to bring back sustenance for the clan. In providing lush delicacies to your loved ones, you're satisfying your hunter genes so that your chosen mates (and let's face it, you're not picky) will survive to bear children.

That instinct cuts both ways. Someone who enjoys and indulges life's joys is far more attractive than a bore who cuts a good figure.

There's something sexual about this, but I cannot for the life of me figure out what.

The American dream. And the British dream. And the Australian dream. Really, just the dream.

That's why a rich and handsome champion athlete like Tom Brady has never seduced any of the women you or I have loved. Wake the gustatory pleasure of a woman's barbecual desire, and you'll be awash in her orange, greasy kisses.

Yes, barbecue boils down to the desire to have it off.

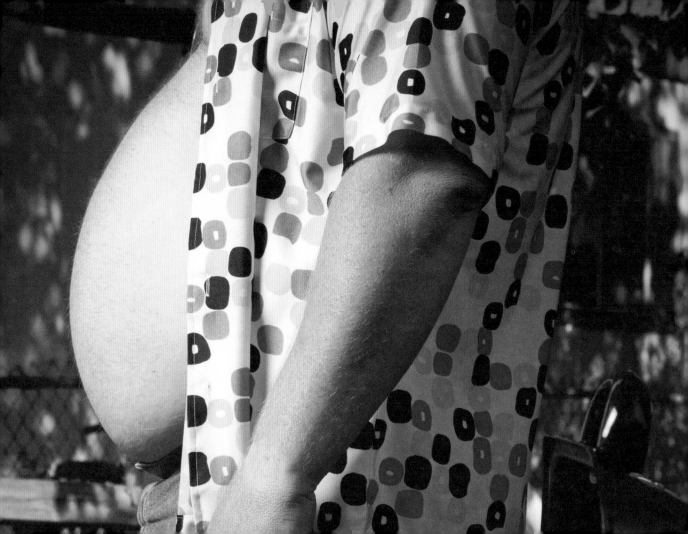

06 NOW WE'RE COOKIN'!

I'll say this again: when the meat's done cooking, leave
it alone for ten minutes. Like the female orgasm, no one
understands it, but it works so long as we believe it will.
Both phenomena function on the placebo effect, named
after its inventor, Dr. Placebo J. Placebo, an Italian
(naturally) who is now wanted in five counties by the law,
and 12 counties by women.

I don't want you getting halfway through the chapter and
sitting down to eat, then blaming me for your failures. I get
enough of that from my family. Just follow my instructions
and you'll soon be even more happily grotesque than this
human hot air balloon to our left.

*That's either a
barbecue gut or the
sun is rising sideways
this morning.*

ESSENTIAL INGREDIENTS THE MYSTERIES OF KITCHEN CUPBOARDS EXPOSED

The heady mix of flavors in barbecue is like assembling an outfit to wear to the ha'penny opera. Whether it's a cummerbund or a dry rub, the elements complement or contrast one another, turning a pile of shabby meat and rich fat into…you. Or possibly a slab of tasty pork ribs, which would be a step up.

The herbs and spices you use will vary widely. Salt is essential, but extracts moisture from the meat, so many cooks add it just before grilling. Ask one of salt's milder friends, like parsley, to hold its place until it's ready to be applied.

CONCERNING LESSER FLAVORS

Sugar comes in many forms, though the ones that concern you are sucrose, glucose, and fructose. These are all the same, which is why they all end in -ose. You may also encounter Galactose, the sugar from beyond!

Acids actually cook the meat a bit, so they may be good to tenderize the piece. Or you can tenderize it the way Rocky did, by hammering it with your bare fists until you're ready to prove to the world that you're not a loser. But what if you are?

Pepper and other hot spices give meat a little kick. Science does not officially recognize burning flesh as a taste, but one day it will, and I'll be there with a Scovillescopometer, waving a map of the heat index drawn in crayon.

Bitterness should be applied sparingly. Good sources of that bitter taste are nutmeg, chicory, or the thought that you've missed your chance to know what love is.

Of course, we all know the only essential ingredient is beer. A good rule of thumb is to drink one beer for every hour that you've wanted a beer.

A "burgerhead son" sounds like a recipe for proud parenting, but how do you resist devouring his face?

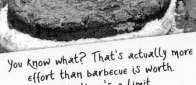

You know what? That's actually more effort than barbecue is worth. Yeah, there's a limit.

SHOW-OFF EDITION
Fancy cheese

Buy some fancy cheese, like Stilton or Brie, and put some in the center of each burger while packing the patties. A cheesy blast of joy now lurks in the middle!

Nice buns! How about a burger?

A great, classic cheeseburger should be in every man's repertoire. Master the basics and then you can add wacky signature ingredients like avocado or despair.

Ingredients

1½ lb rib-eye steak, ground
1 onion, finely chopped
1 garlic clove, crushed like your dreams
2 tsp chopped thyme
olive oil, for sexy, sexy brushing
4 oz Cheddar cheese, grated
4 burger buns, halved
4 large lettuce leaves
2 tomatoes, sliced
salt and black pepper

SERVES 4
Prep time: 15 mins, plus 30 mins chilling
Cooking time: 10–12 mins

Method

1 Put the steak, onion, garlic, thyme, and some salt and pepper in a bowl. Use your hands to work them together until evenly combined and slightly sticky. Divide the mixture into quarters and shape into 4 even-sized burger shapes. Chill for 30 minutes.

2 Brush the raw burgers with a little oil, and cook on a hot barbecue for 5–6 minutes on each side, until cooked through and lightly charred on the outside. Top with cheese, and place under a hot grill for 30 seconds until melted.

3 Meanwhile, toast the buns on the barbecue for 1 minute on the cut side. Fill each bun with lettuce leaves, cheese-topped burgers and tomato slices.

Top dogs

These are a kissing cousin to the world famous Chicago-style dogs, which eschew barbecue and swap thyme for dill. I recommend you try both—dogs that is, not kissing your cousin.

Ingredients
2 large onions, sliced
2 tbsp extra virgin olive oil
1 tbsp chopped thyme
4 large pork sausages
4 hot dog rolls, halved
butter for rolls
salt and black pepper
4 tbsp barbecue sauce for drizzling (see *Show-off Edition*, right)

SERVES 4
Prep time: 10 mins
Cooking time: 15–20 mins

Method
1 Toss the onions with the oil, thyme, salt and pepper, then cook on a ridged grill over a hot barbecue for 15–20 minutes. If you're using a propane barbecue, cook these on the flat plate, but don't expect any compliments.
2 Meanwhile, cook the sausages on the barbecue until they're lightly charred and cooked through (about 10 minutes).
3 Butter the bread rolls and fill with the sausages and onions. Drizzle with barbecue sauce—use a homemade version to impress a hot date or soothe a sulky wife. A little drizzle on the shirt is compulsory. Or do it Chicago-style and serve the onions raw, swapping bbq sauce with ketchup.

Date

SHOW-OFF EDITION
Homemade barbecue sauce

8 fl oz tomato purée
4 fl oz treacle
3 fl oz maple syrup
3 fl oz white wine vinegar
2 tbsp Worcestershire sauce
1 tbsp Dijon mustard
1 tsp garlic powder
¼ tsp smoked paprika
salt and black pepper

Place all the ingredients in a pan and heat gently until bubbling. Lower the heat and simmer gently for 10–15 minutes until the sauce thickens slightly, then transfer to a fancy bowl.

Nuance is everything. The way this Sicilian holds his burger indicates he has marked it for death. ⇨

SHOW-OFF EDITION
Leaf it alone
Go crazy. Place a basil leaf on the stick too, if you like. Resist the temptation to go further. Don't overstep your authority.

Scary Sicilian burgers

Archimedes himself designed these burgers. Careful with the sun-dried tomatoes. They taste great, but a little of their flavor goes a long way.

Ingredients

1 tbsp olive oil, plus extra for brushing
1 red onion, finely chopped
3 garlic cloves, finely chopped
1¼ lb good quality, coarsely ground beef
2 tbsp chopped basil
2 tbsp chopped marjoram
2 tbsp chopped oregano
2 oz freshly grated Parmesan cheese
3 oz sun-dried tomatoes, finely chopped
3 oz black olives, finely chopped
2 soft focaccia rolls, quartered, then halved
mayonnaise
6–8 arugula or lettuce leaves
1 ball mozzarella cheese (about 4 oz)
salt and black pepper

SERVES 4
Prep time: 20 mins, plus 30 mins chilling
Cooking time: 12–14 mins

Method

1 Heat the oil in a skillet, then fry the onion and garlic over a medium heat for 4 minutes or until softened. Set aside to cool.

2 Place the beef, onion and garlic mixture, herbs, Parmesan, tomatoes, and olives into a large bowl, season with salt and pepper, and mix well. Divide the mixture into 8, and shape into 8 burger-shaped pieces. Cover and chill for 30 minutes.

3 Brush the raw burgers with a little oil and cook on a hot barbecue for 4–5 minutes on each side until slightly charred on the outside and medium in the center.

4 Meanwhile, toast the halved focaccia quarters on the barbecue over indirect heat until browned—each side needs less than a minute.

5 Spread the base of each bun with some mayonnaise (mix in some chopped basil for bonus style points), then place the arugula/lettuce and burger on top. Tear the mozzarella into 8 pieces, and place some on top of each burger. Finish by topping each one with a toasted focaccia lid. You should now have a burger bigger than your face. Pin the burger together with a cocktail stick—or act like you're the man and try to hold it together. Aim for nonchalance.

Rib ticklers

This is the consummate barbecue dish. Prep these ribs on a rainy Saturday night and spend a lovely Sunday slow-cooking them.

Ingredients
2 lb pork spare rib rack
1 tbsp olive oil, plus extra for brushing
4 tbsp smoky barbecue rub
(buy or make—see page 123)
16 fl oz barbecue sauce
(buy or make—see page 119)

SERVES 4
Prep time: 20 mins, plus marinating overnight
Cooking time: 2–8 hours

Method
1 Mix the oil and barbecue rub together and rub this all over the ribs. Cover and marinate in the refrigerator overnight.
2 In the morning, lightly heat the barbecue sauce.
3 Remove the ribs from the dish, brush with a little extra oil, then sear over an open flame for 5–10 minutes on each side to develop a crunchy exterior. Remove them from the heat and wrap in aluminum foil (the ribs, you fool).
4 Rake the hot coals away from the center of the grate to the side, and then place the foil-wrapped ribs above the cool spot. Close the barbecue, and cook the rib rack for...oh my, hours and hours—around 6 to 8, depending on the size of the rack and how low in temperature you go.
5 Remove the foil and put the ribs directly over the now low-to-medium heat. Baste with barbecue sauce, and remove when it has caramelized enough to become thicker and stickier. Remove from the heat and let sit a few minutes before cutting. Savor the moment.

High steaks

The whole point of this recipe is the flavored butter, a favorite trick of steakhouses. And yeah, it'll be delicious, but I often feel it's gilding the lily. A good steak should speak for itself. In my belly. But some days you're going to want hedonism.

Ingredients

4 T-bone steaks, about 1 lb each
1½ tbsp chopped thyme
2 tbsp extra virgin olive oil
salt and black pepper
4 oz garlic and herb butter
  (buy or make—see *Show-off Edition*, left)

SERVES 4
Prep time: 10 mins
Cooking time: 10 mins

Method

1 Season the steaks with salt, pepper, and thyme, and rub them with oil. Admire.
2 Cook on a hot barbecue for 5 minutes on each side, then wrap loosely in foil and set aside to rest for 5 minutes. Serve each one topped with a slice of the butter. Easy.

SHOW-OFF EDITION
Homemade herby garlic butter

4 oz butter
1 garlic clove, crushed
2 tbsp drained capers
1 tbsp chopped parsley

Put the ingredients into a bowl and season to taste. Shape into a log, wrap in food wrap, and chill until required. When the steaks are ready, casually place a slice of the butter onto each one as though you always do this.

This isn't preparing steaks; it's a blood-orgy.

Happy hog-day sandwich

If you don't have the time and giant oven to pull your own Carolina-style 10-lb pork leg, try this version for a sammich that'll turn the bread into glue and your pantry into nirvana.

Ingredients

2 tbsp smoky barbecue rub (buy or make—see Show-off Edition, right)
2 lb boneless pork shoulder
8 bread rolls

SERVES 8
Prep time: 45 mins, plus 6–10 hours marinating
Cooking time: 1–1¼ hours

Method

1 Rub your smoky barbecue rub all over the pork and leave to marinate overnight in the refrigerator. Return the pork to room temperature for 1 hour before cooking.

2 Cook the pork by the indirect grilling method on a medium barbecue for 1–1¼ hours until tender. Wrap loosely in foil and set aside to rest for 15 minutes. Have a beer.

3 Finely slice the pork and serve in rolls with some coleslaw made by your lovely wife. Or buy some. Who cares? It's only vegetables.

SHOW-OFF EDITION
Smoky barbecue rub

Date

There are so many craft rubs, you might as well save time and buy one, passing it off as your own. On the other hand, the sheer number means the decision-making may be more arduous than simply rubbing together these sweet-smelling, spicy powders.

1 tbsp salt
1 tbsp smoked paprika
1 tsp ground coriander
2 tsp crushed black pepper
2 tsp mustard powder
1 tsp caster sugar
¼ tsp cayenne pepper

Combine all the ingredients and mix well. Wooah! Tiring.

Hot and spicy birds

Maybe spicy isn't quite the word. These chicken drumsticks are going to be really herby, with pow, zip, pop, and other elements that used to be the names of 1960s gossip magazines.

Ingredients

1 garlic clove
2 inch piece of fresh ginger root, peeled and chopped
juice and finely grated rind of 2 limes
2 tbsp light soy sauce
2 tbsp groundnut oil
2 tsp ground cinnamon
1 tsp ground turmeric
2 tbsp clear honey
8 chicken drumsticks
salt

SERVES 4
Prep time: 10 mins, plus 1–6 hours marinating
Cooking time: 20 mins

Method

1 Place everything except the chicken in a blender or food processor, and blend until smooth. That's the marinade done.

2 Put the chicken drumsticks in a shallow dish, pour the marinade over the top and toss the sticks in a whimsical way until they're coated. Cover and leave to marinate for 1–6 hours.

3 Remove the chicken from the marinade, and cook the pieces on a medium hot barbecue, turning every 3 minutes or so, for around 20 minutes. Test the chicken is cooked by checking there is no trace of pink at the bone. If you're uncertain, have someone you don't like eat a test piece. If they become ill, that was a bad piece.

This is way too wholesome to really be barbecue.

SHOW-OFF EDITION

SHOW-OFF EDITION
Lime aïoli

4–6 garlic cloves, crushed
2 egg yolks
juice and finely grated rind of 2 limes
½ pint extra virgin olive oil

Place the garlic and egg yolks in a food processor or blender, add the lime juice, then process briefly to mix. Now for the tricky part. With the machine running, gradually add the olive oil in a thin, steady stream until the mixture forms a thick cream. If this works first time, consider yourself a genius. Turn the aïoli into a bowl, stir in the lime rind, and season with some salt and pepper if you want. Kind of like tartar sauce, isn't it? You're welcome.

99 per cent of all marine life's encounters with fire are due to human tastebuds.

See? Bass!

Fish loves a good citric acid, like the lime in this recipe, because it sets off its inherent briny taste. Capers are nice, too. Really, anything tart is a smart match, which is why I always order fish when I date your sister. Zing!

Ingredients

4 large potatoes, scrubbed
4 tbsp olive oil
4 sea bass fillets, 6–8 oz each
salt and black pepper
aïoli (buy or make—see *Show-off Edition, left*); if you're buying ready-made aïoli, buy 2 fresh limes too

SERVES 4
Prep time: 30 mins
Cooking time: 18–20 mins

Garnish to impress

grilled lime slices
snipped chives

Method

1 If you're making aïoli, do it now. If you've bought some, squeeze the juice from the 2 limes into the aïoli, and grate in a little of the lime rind. Now it's homemade.

2 Slice the potatoes thinly and brush well with olive oil. Sprinkle the slices with salt and pepper and cook on a hot barbecue for 8–10 minutes on each side until tender and golden. Remove from the heat and keep warm.

3 Score the sea bass fillets, brush well with the remaining olive oil, and cook, skin side down, on the barbecue for 3–4 minutes until just cooked, turning once. Remove from the heat and serve the fish, potatoes, and aïoli—garnishing the plates of VIPs with lime slices and chives.

Billy the Squid with hot chili jam

American engineering has reduced the number of Ls in the British word "chilli" to a highly efficient solitary letter. The implicit danger is that if your tongue stumbles, you have no secondary L to fall back on, and the whole word crashes.

SERVES 4
Prep time: 15 mins, plus 15 mins marinating
Cooking time: 1–2 mins

Ingredients
2 lb cleaned squid
2–4 garlic cloves, crushed
1 tbsp sea salt
1 tbsp light brown soft sugar
chili jam (buy or make— see Show-off Edition, right);
lime wedges, to garnish

Method
1 Remove the tentacles from inside the squid bodies and slice the tentacles away from the beak part of the head. If you haven't fainted yet, remove the quill from inside each body, if present. Steady yourself with a beer.
2 Cut the bodies in half lengthways and then crossways, then use a sharp knife to score the inside with a diamond pattern. Place the squid pieces in a bowl. Add the garlic, salt, and sugar, rub in well, then leave to marinate for 15 minutes.
3 Cook the squid on a hot barbecue for 1–2 minutes, garnish with lime wedges, and serve with the chili jam.

SHOW-OFF EDITION
Chili jam

Date

Buy some chili jam and decant to a bowl, passing it off as your own, or go crazy and actually make your own. But don't be tempted if you're rushed for time—this takes about an hour to make. Time better spent chatting up ladies. Or, hey, impress them by making this before their very eyes.

4 bird's-eye chilis
1 lb tomatoes
2 garlic cloves, crushed
6 oz light brown sugar
4 fl oz red wine vinegar
salt and black pepper

Place all the ingredients in a pan, bring the mixture to the boil, and simmer for 45 minutes until thickened and jam-like. Leave to cool completely.

Shrimply the best

A shrimp's a nice, simple critter. Chop here, peel there, strip therein, and you're done. Shrimp really respond to a spectrum of flavors. They're the candy of the sea. Skittering, primordial bug candy. Yum!

Ingredients
12 Dublin Bay shrimp, thawed if frozen, peeled with tails left on, deveined
8 streaky bacon slices, rind removed, halved lengthways and rolled up

SERVES 4
Prep time: 10 mins, plus 1 hour marinating
Cooking time: 6-8 mins

Balsamic marinade
5 tbsp olive oil
2 tbsp balsamic vinegar
2 tbsp chopped oregano or marjoram
2 garlic cloves, crushed
black pepper

Method
1 Mix all the marinade ingredients in a shallow bowl. Add the shrimp to the marinade, turning to coat thoroughly. Cover and leave to marinate for 1 hour.
2 Drain the shrimp, reserving the marinade, and thread them on to 4 metal skewers, alternating with the rolled-up bacon. Yeah, it's messy.
3 Cook on a hot barbecue for 6-8 minutes, turning the skewers several times and brushing the shrimp and bacon with the remaining marinade, until the shrimp are tender and cooked through, the bacon is crisp, and you've had time to consider what went wrong last night.
4 Serve with your carb of choice. Rice and peas are good, but bread is easier.

There's one! Spear it!

SHOW-OFF EDITION
You just did it.

ACKNOWLEDGMENTS

Commissioning Editor: Trevor Davies
Art Director: Tracy Killick
Managing Editor: Sarah Tomley
Designer: Paul Palmer-Edwards at
   Grade Design
Picture Researchers: Giulia Hetherington
   and Jennifer Veall
Production Manager: Peter Hunt

Produced for Octopus Publishing Group
by Tracy Killick Art Direction and Design
67 Ross Road, Surrey SM6 8QP;
www.tracykillick.co.uk

Author's Acknowledgments
Thank you to Sarah for hiring me, and
to my brother-in-law Mike for teaching
me what steak on the grill could be.

Photographic Acknowledgments

Advertising Archives 94 centre

akg-images Dodenhoff 18

Alamy Ace Stock Limited 2; ClassicStock/H Armstrong Roberts 21 above; Full Picture 71 above; Jinny Goodman 7 below; John T Fowler 100; Matt Child 24 below; Ola Lundqvist 105; Peter Dench 71 below; RF Company 15; Sodapix 70 above; Stock Connection Blue 103

Corbis Bettmann 8, 77 above; Brooke Fasani Auchincloss 112; Franz-Marc Frei 110 right; Greg Smith 23; H Armstrong Roberts/ClassicStock 65; Hill Street Studios/Blend Images 61; Historical Picture Archive 12; Howell Walker/National Geographic Society 88; Kevin Fleming 76 above; Lawrence Manning 120; Michael Freeman 11; Norbert Wu/Science Faction 24 above; Parque 89; PNC 83; Robert Recker 62 above, 113 right; Wolfgang Deuter 16 above

David Klose BBQ Pits by Klose, david@bbqpits.com, www.bbqpits.com, toll free 1-800-487-7487 42

Fotolia Alexander Maksimenko 25 below; Beboy 10; Chris Mautz 14 above; Christopher Howey 119; Gratien Jonxis 25 above; Hellen Sergeyeva 104; Lasse Kristensen 94 above; tdoes 121; Valeriy Kirsanov 77 below

Fotosearch 48

Getty Images 79, 52 below; AFP 122; Baerbel Schmidt 27; Bob Elsdale 7 above; Burazin 22; Burke/Triolo Productions 13; Constance Bannister Corp 14 below; David Zaitz 90; Diana Koenigsberg 107; Diane Collins and Jordan Hollender 92; Digital Vision 97 above; Edward Holub 76 below; Eg Project 16 below; Hugh Kretschmer 58; Jay P Morgan 117; Jupiterimages 98; Karan Kapoor 113 left; Lambert 62 below; Loungepark 97 below; Mark Klotz 84; Matthias Clamer 66; Mike Kemp 86; Nick Daly 70 below; Nisian Hughes 31 left; Nivek Neslo 17; Peter Mason 102; Petri Artturi Asikainen 5; Philip Lee Harvey 101; Sarah Leen 39 left; Science & Society Picture Library 108; Sean Murphy 51; Steffen Thalemann 93; SuperStock 124 above & below; Thomas Northcut 111; Time & Life Pictures 80, /Ed Clarke 52 above, /Burton McNeely 41 left & right; Todd Warnock 87; Tom Schierlitz 123; Travel Ink 57, 126; Ulf Huett Nilsson 31 inset; Vintage Images 53; WIN-Initiative 110 left

Joel Haas 35 left & right

Lonely Planet Images Tim Barker 127

Paul Heavisides 47

Photolibrary Group Corbis 4 right; Curt Teich Postcard Archives 21 below; Daniel J Cox 94 below; Frances Andrijich 32; Johner Bildbyra 6; Kablonk! 73; Mike Kemp 114

Rex Features 36; Assignments Photographers 54, 55; KPA/Zuma 118

SuperStock 44, 69; Corbis 74; Fotosearch 39 right; Francisco Cruz 106

Terry Smith PlanoHomesandLand.com 29

Tim Linder 28

Backgrounds and incidental images courtesy of cgtextures.com and Cobalt/fotolia.com; Hawkeye/fotolia.com; Maxim Loskutnikov/fotolia.com; rufar/fotolia.com